GREAT PETS

Parrots

Johannah Haney

 **Marshall Cavendish**
Benchmark
New York

For Putifar, the Choroy parrot from Chile

Marshall Cavendish Benchmark
99 White Plains Road
Tarrytown, New York 10591
www.marshallcavendish.us

Library of Congress Cataloging-in-Publication Data

Haney, Johannah.
Parrots / by Johannah Haney.
p. cm. -- (Great pets)
Includes bibliographical references and index.
Summary: "Describes the characteristics and behavior of pet parrots, also
discussing their physical appearance and place in history"--Provided by publisher.
ISBN 978-0-7614-2998-2
1. Parrots--Juvenile literature. I. Title.
SF473.P3H36 2008
636.6'865--dc22
2008024335

Front cover: An African grey
Title page: Macaws
Back cover: An Amazon parrot and a cockatoo

Photo research by Candlepants, Inc.
Front cover: Biosphoto/Jardel C. & Labat J.-M/ Peter Arnold Inc.
The photographs in this book are used by permission and through the courtesy of:
Photo Researchers, Inc.: Kathy Davey, 10, 15, 18; Cindy George, 20, 38; Exotic Wings Canada, 23, 28; Carolyn A.
McKeone, 31; Tracey Charleson, 43; Dale Hauk, 44. Corbis: B. Mathur/Reuters, 1; H. Takano/zefa, 7, back cover; Theo
Allofs, 12, 22; Jim Craigmyle, 40. Art Resource: Werner Forman, 4. Alamy: Juniors Bildarchiv, 8, 34; Petra Wegner, 30.
Getty Images: AFP, 13; GK Hart/Vikki Hart, 16; VEER Renee DeMartin, 19; Patrick Byrd, 27; Altrendo Nature, 39.
SuperStock: Mary Evans Picture Library/The Image Works, 6; age footstock, 21, 24. Shutterstock: Dee Hunter, 26;
Jasenka Luksa, 33; Susan Harris, 36.

Editor: Karen Ang
Publisher: Michelle Bisson
Art Director: Anahid Hamparian
Series Design by: Elynn Cohen

Printed in Malaysia
6 5 4 3 2 1

Contents

1

All about Parrots

Different types of parrots have flown through the skies for millions of years. Fossils found in England have shown parrots lived in that region around forty million years ago. Their vivid colors and amazing ability to **mimic** sound and speech have made parrots irresistible pets for thousands of years. Ancient Egyptians used images of parrots in their hieroglyphics, or way of writing. Ancient Greeks, and later the Romans, kept pet parrots in cages made of precious metals like gold.

When European explorers traveled to North, Central, and South America in the late 1400s, they began to bring the most colorful and exotic

Ancient cultures that lived in the area that now includes Mexico valued parrots for their brightly colored feathers. Some used stone carvings of macaws for their sacred ball games.

Many pirates in legends and stories were said to have pet parrots that perched on their shoulders.

parrots back to Europe. These birds were sold as pets, especially to royalty and to wealthy Europeans. In fact, the demand for pet parrots in Europe might be why parrots are associated with pirates. Sailors brought parrots from the Americas on their ships, and sailed them across the Atlantic as their traveling companions. When they arrived, they sold the parrots as pets or kept them.

Many poets have written that parrots look as though they have flown through a rainbow. Not only are parrots beautiful, but many can be trained to speak, finish simple puzzles, put coins in a piggybank, and recognize colors. Parrots also live very long lives—sometimes as long as eighty years. This makes keeping a pet parrot a very long and serious commitment.

Parrots can be wonderful pets, but they are not necessarily right for every home.

Is a Parrot Right for You?

Bringing home any kind of pet requires careful thought and planning. Some pet parrots can cost a lot of money. A parrot needs a spacious cage, special food, toys, and visits to a **veterinarian.** Buying a parrot can sometimes cost a lot of money too, depending on the type of parrot you want. Some parrots, such as budgerigars and cockatiels may cost around $30 to $100.

Cockatiels are some of the most popular pet parrots.

However, larger parrots, like a macaw or an African grey, can cost $1,500 or more. Yearly costs for food, vet care, toys, and other supplies may also be very expensive.

PRESIDENTIAL PARROTS

United States presidents Andrew Jackson, Ulysses S. Grant, William McKinley, Theodore Roosevelt, and Calvin Coolidge each kept pet parrots. When President McKinley whistled the beginning notes of "Yankee Doodle," his pet parrot whistled the rest of the tune.

People are sometimes surprised about how loud pet parrots can be. Most parrots are naturally noisy and will often make noise all day and even into the evening. A parrot's ability to mimic sound makes it a very interesting and fun pet, but remember that some parrots will mimic any sounds they hear often. They might repeat words you are teaching them, but these birds may also mimic sounds like car alarms, police sirens, ringing phones, crying babies, or even barking dogs!

Parrots are naturally curious and active. In order to be healthy and happy, a pet parrot needs a lot of attention and time with its human. Many parrot owners compare having a large parrot to having a small child because of all the attention the parrot needs.

Despite the time, money, and effort involved, people continue to keep parrots as pets. One reason is because these smart animals can form a close bond with their humans. They are beautiful to look at and fun to play with. Pet parrots can provide their owners with many years of companionship and joy.

2

Choosing Your Parrot

There are several places to find a pet parrot. One place is a **breeder**—someone who raises and sells parrots. Another place where you can find parrots is at a parrot rescue organization. When people can no longer care for their pet parrot, they might give the parrot to a rescue organization to find it a good home. Many people buy their parrots from pet stores. Some pet stores sell only parrots and other birds. Regular pet stores usually carry a variety of parrots, especially budgerigars, or "budgies."

Pet parrots that you adopt or buy should have been hatched in captivity and have spent their lives around humans. A bird that is

There are many different breeds of parrots to choose from. Amazon parrots, like this lilac-crowned one, come in different sizes, colors, and personalities.

Pet stores, breeders, and parrot rescue organizations have many different types of birds from which to choose. There should be no reason to catch wild birds to be kept as pets.

hatched in captivity means that it was not captured from the wild. Breeders who raise parrots from the time they hatch will often say their birds are "hand fed" or "hand raised." This means that the breeder has fed the baby birds every couple of hours, as the bird's natural parent might do. Many people feel that hand-raised birds tend to be more friendly and easier to handle. You can often find hand-raised birds at pet stores.

Things to Look for

When you are picking out a parrot you want to make sure you get a healthy pet. The first thing you need to look at is the place where you are getting the parrot. If you are adopting a parrot from a rescue organization you can do some research to find out more. Most rescue organizations have Web sites or printed flyers or brochures that provide information. Some questions you can ask include how long has the organization been around, who

You should carefully examine the parrot and where it is kept before you adopt or buy it.

are its volunteers, what kind of birds do they rescue and place in homes, and are there references from people who are happy with their adopted birds? Do people working there seem to know a lot about their parrots and how to take care of them? You can also ask the same questions when you are buying a bird from a breeder.

Whether you go to a rescue organization, a breeder, or a pet store, you want to make sure the birds' surroundings are clean. Does the place where

Wild Birds

Parrots that were caught in the wild should never be bought or sold as pets. In fact, it is illegal to catch a wild parrot for a pet. Wild parrots that are sold as pets have been taken from their homes and forced to live in cages they are not familiar with. They will most likely be unhappy, and could also be unhealthy.

Exotic pet auctions also sometimes sell parrots, but it is difficult to know where the parrots sold at auctions come from, and whether or not they will be good pets. Do not be afraid to ask the breeder or pet store for some proof of where the parrot comes from. Responsible parrot sellers will be happy to give you this information.

the birds are kept look clean? Are there a lot of feathers or bird waste littering the area? Do the cages look clean? Are there a lot of birds stuffed into a small cage? Do the birds have space to move around inside their cages? Does it look like they are fed regularly? Healthy birds are kept in a clean environment that has clean water, available food, and plenty of space to move around.

What about the bird you want? Does it look like it is happy and healthy? Are its eyes clear and alert? Does the bird look like it is having a hard time breathing? (Parrots that appear to work hard in order to take a breath may be sick.) How do its feathers look? In general, the bird should be covered in clean and smooth feathers. Some birds will look raggedy when they are **molting,** so be sure to ask if that is the case. Is it moving around its cage? Does it chatter or make noise? Does it fly or climb away when you approach the cage? If it is a bird that is used to being handled, ask to carefully hold it. Does the bird not like to be touched?

Careful research will help you choose the parrot that is perfect for you.

Getting answers to these questions will help you decide where to get your bird. However, before you buy a bird, be sure to do research about the different types and what kind would best suit your home.

3

Types of Parrots

There are more than three hundred different species—or types—of parrots in the wild and in captivity. All parrots have wings, a beak, a tail, and four toes on each foot. Two of the toes point to the front and two point to the back. This helps them grasp onto tree branches or perches. Parrots also use their beaks to help them climb. Parrots' beaks are shaped like a hook and are very strong. This strength allows them to break open tough seeds and other food. Beaks are also used for playing and **preening,** which means cleaning their feathers. All parrots have these features, but depending upon their breed and size, the features may vary slightly.

Most pet cockatoos have white feathers. Some types, however, can be pink, grey, peach, or a mix of these colors.

African Greys

These parrots are mostly grey in color. Their feathers are a mixture of white and grey. The spots of color in these parrots are on their faces, and tails. The eyes usually are yellow in adult African greys, with white around the eyes and nostrils. Some African greys usually live between fifty to sixty years, sometimes longer. They grow to be about 13 inches (33 centimeters) long, and they are very strong birds.

Though they are not as colorful as macaws, African greys are among the most intelligent parrots. Many enjoy doing simple puzzles. African greys are

Parrots like African greys need toys and games to keep their minds active.

also known for their mimicry skills. Some say that these parrots are the best at mimicking sounds and words. Like all large parrots, African greys need an enormous amount of attention and care.

Amazons

Amazons are very good at imitating the sounds they hear around them. They can live between 25 years to 80 years, and most grow to be about 15 inches

Some families might consider getting two pet parrots. Not all parrots get along, however, and parrots that are kept together might not bond as closely with their human caretakers.

(38 cm) long. Amazons can be very colorful. Many have green and yellow feathers on their bodies, with colorful spots on their heads or shoulders. For example, the blue-fronted Amazon is mostly green with blue feathers around its beak, and yellow and red patches on its shoulders. Red-Lored Amazons have vivid red feathers on their lore—or forehead—and a blue crown. Amazons need a lot of space, toys to keep them occupied, and a lot of human attention.

Budgerigars

Often called "budgies" or parakeets, these birds are very common pets. Budgies usually grow to be about 7 inches (18 cm) long and live around seven to ten years. Budgies interact well with humans and other budgies, but do not get along well with other bird species.

Some budgies, especially males, can be quite good at mimicking words and sounds. A budgie named Puck was in the Guinness Book of World Records for being the bird with the largest vocabulary in the

Budgies are very popular pet parrots because of their size and sweet personalities.

world. Puck could say 1,728 words! Even budgies that do not talk tend to chatter and chirp a lot. Budgies do not require as much space and are less expensive than a larger parrot. However, they still need a lot of attention from their humans.

Cockatoos

Depending on their type and age, cockatoos can range from 12 inches (30 cm) to 20 inches (50 cm) long. Most cockatoos have a large tuft of feathers—called a **crest**—sitting right on top of their heads. (Cockatoos control their crests and either have them flat against their heads or raised up.) Most cockatoos are white with colored crests. For example, the sulfur-crested cockatoo has a yellow crest on its head. Moluccan cockatoos have peach- or pink-tinted feathers with brighter reddish feathers in their crests. Cockatoos can live for more then thirty years and need plenty of space.

Cockatoos sometimes raise their crests when they are curious or happy.

Cockatiels

These small parrots are one of the most popular breeds. Cockatiels are a type of cockatoo, and also have distinctive crests at the tops of their heads. Cockatiels are about 10 inches (25 cm) long. They can be white, yellow, gray, or a mix of all of these colors. Most cockatiels have bright reddish orange patches of color on each of their cheeks.

Cockatiels make excellent pets for the first-time parrot owner. They are not too big, can be easy to handle, and are fun to keep. Cockatiels can be taught to whistle tunes, and many can even speak a few words.

Conures

Nanday, Jendaya, and Senegal, and Sun conures are the most common types of parrot pets in this species. Conures can be a rainbow of colors, from bright green to fiery red and orange with flecks of blue or black. Some conures are about 10 inches (25 cm) long, and usually live around twenty years. They are smart, loving, and often very noisy birds.

Sun conures have feathers of many different bold and bright colors.

This black-capped lory enjoys a snack of fresh fruit.

Lories and Lorikeets

These birds are colorful and playful, but can sometimes be messy pets. The dusky lory is about 10 inches (25 cm) long and has red, yellow, and orange flecks with shades of green or brown. These birds can live around thirty years. Red lories are, as their name suggests, bright red, and are about 12 inches (30 cm). The rainbow lorikeet is vividly colored and lives fifteen to twenty-five years. Lories and lorikeets of all types are usually playful. Since lories and lorikeets eat nectar, pollen, and fruit in the wild, they need a mostly liquid diet with some fruits and vegetables.

Lovebirds

Smaller birds at just 6 inches (15 cm), lovebirds are very popular pets. Different types of lovebirds include the peach-faced, Fischer's, and masked

Two peach-faced lovebirds snuggle together on their perch.

lovebirds. The lifespan varies for different types, but is usually around fifteen years. Lovebirds make excellent pets, but if you have a lovebird it is best to keep just lovebirds, because they can become aggressive toward—or are likely to attack—other parrot species.

Macaws

When people think of parrots, many picture macaws. That is because macaws are some of the largest and most colorful pet parrots. Macaws vary

BANDED BIRDS

Often, parrots will be banded, which means there is a small metal ring around one leg that identifies the bird. Because the band will only fit over the foot of a very young parrot, a banded bird is usually a sign that the bird was hatched in captivity. This band is meant to stay around the bird's leg for life. In most cases, it is not uncomfortable for the animal and never causes problems. It might also help you identify your pet bird if it accidentally flies outside.

Because of their size and the amount of care they need, some breeders feel that most macaws are not the right choice for first-time parrot owners.

in size, from the Hahn macaw, which grows to be about 13 inches (33 cm) to the scarlet macaw which can be 36 inches (91 cm). A macaw's life span is forty to eighty years or longer. Because macaws are naturally curious, they need a lot of activity and toys to keep them happy.

The popularity of this species has encouraged some people to capture wild macaws to sell as pets. As a result, the populations of wild macaws have become dangerously low. It is only legal to buy macaws that have been born in captivity.

If you are not sure what kind of parrot suits you, do some more research. Talk to different breeders or pet store workers. Ask if you can carefully handle a few different types to see how you feel. Do not be afraid to take your time when deciding on a parrot species. Choosing a feathered friend is an important decision that should be carefully considered.

A lory carefully grooms his human friend during playtime.

4

Parrot Care

Like all pets, parrots need food and water, someone to clean up after them, and a lot of attention and affection. Parrots also need their humans to help keep them healthy and safe in their homes.

Cages

Parrots need a cage that is big enough for them to live happily. Parrots in the wild can fly up to 30 miles each day. Although it is impossible to provide such an environment for pet parrots, giving your pet the most amount of safe space possible is the right thing to do. You should buy the biggest

With the proper supplies, hard work, and patience, you can have a happy and healthy pet parrot.

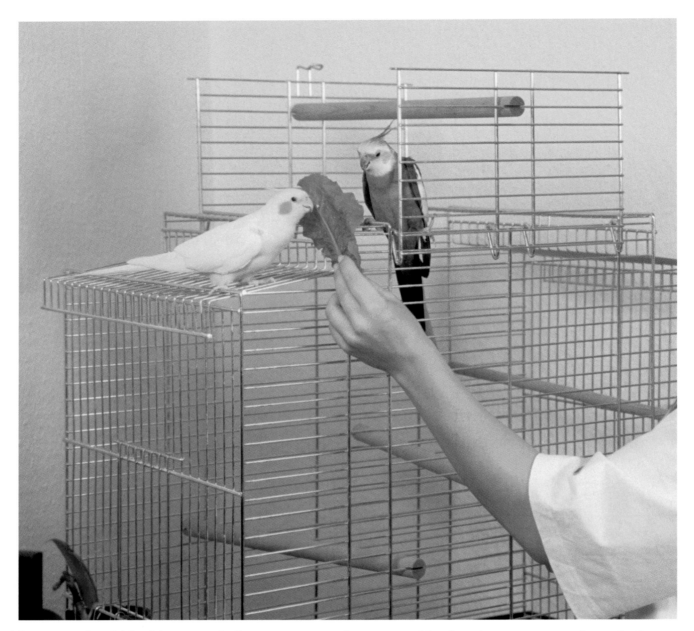

The cage should be big enough for your parrot, but not so big that it can escape through the bars. If you have more than one parrot in a cage, be sure that they each have enough space to move around.

cage you can for your type of parrot. Be sure, however, that the spaces between the bars of the cage are not big enough for your bird to squeeze through. Some parrots get their heads or shoulders stuck when trying to squeeze between bars that are a too wide. The sturdiest cages are made from metal. Some types of metals are poisonous to parrots, so make sure your parrot's cage is made from stainless steel.

Parrots are very intelligent animals. Some have been known to learn how the latch on their cage door works so they can open it themselves! Make sure the latch on the cage door is secure. Some parrot owners even use a lock so their parrots cannot break out of the cage.

Each day you should make sure your bird spends time outside of its cage. The cage, however, will be where your bird will spend most of its time. This is why it is important that the cage is set up properly. Your bird should be able to climb around the cage easily. Place a

Small birds, such as budgies, like having mirrors in their cages. Some breeders, however, do not recommend mirrors for larger parrots.

few perches—at different sizes and heights—around the cage. There should be an area specifically for your bird's food and water. Toys can also be placed inside the cage.

The cage should be lined with newspaper at the bottom to collect discarded seeds, shells, or other food scraps. Parrots will also go to bathroom in their cage. These droppings will fall to the bottom lined with paper. Replace the newspaper every day, and clean the cage often. Cages, perches, and toys can be washed with warm water and soap, but be sure to rinse away all of the soap.

Wild parrots have a variety of interesting things to see in their natural habitat. Pet parrots are just as interested in their surroundings. Keep your parrot's cage in a common room at home so it can watch people come and go and observe a lot of activity. Make sure, however, that the cage is not too close to a window or door. Drafts of cold air from these openings can make your bird uncomfortable or sick. Doors and windows are also a dangerous escape route for your pet parrots.

Parrot Safety

When you let your parrot out of its cage, make sure there is nothing in your house that can harm it. Parrots naturally chew on anything they can, so make sure electrical wires and cords are tucked away. When your parrot is allowed out of its cage, make sure there are no ceiling fans running, and that the stovetop is off. Lead, a metal that is toxic to humans if swallowed, is also very harmful to parrots. Make sure there are no lead-based paint chips or other lead items your parrot can swallow. Make sure your parrot is safe from curious dogs or cats, or excited children who may accidentally hurt it.

Feeding

Parrots need a wide variety of food in order to get all the vitamins and minerals they need to stay healthy. Pet stores offer parrot food in the form of

Most parrots enjoy sweet treats like strawberries or other fresh fruit.

pellets and seed. But some parrots also need a wide range of table food—such as sweet potatoes, tomatoes, grapes, carrots, pomegranate, broccoli, lean meat, rice, lettuce, and melon—to get all the nutrients they need. Not all human food is good for your parrot. Avocadoes and chocolate are both poisonous to parrots. Fried food, caffeine, and large quantities of sugar and salt are also not healthy for parrots.

Many people think parrots eat mainly seeds. In fact, seeds offer very limited nutrition and are high in fat, so seeds should be used only as a special treat. Parrots also love many types of nuts. Nuts provide parrots with protein and energy, as well as other nutrients like iron and calcium. Nuts still in the shell provide larger parrots with a fun job as they crack open shells to find the prize inside. A veterinarian or breeder can help you determine what is good for your parrot.

Parrots need a constant source of fresh drinking water. Large

Smaller birds may prefer to drink their water from special water bottles that hang from the side of the cage.

parrots prefer water bowls that are wide and shallow. Be sure to change the food and water whenever there are droppings inside the bowls. The food and water dishes should also be cleaned regularly with soap and water.

Parrot Health

A parrot's respiratory tract—the body system in charge of breathing—is very sensitive. Many household cleaners and other items can be harmful to a parrot's respiratory tract. If you use these kinds of cleaners, be sure your parrot is kept away where it cannot breathe in these chemicals. Some parrot owners use homemade cleaners, such as baking soda mixed with water. Non-stick surfaces on cookware give off fumes when they become too hot, and these fumes are poisonous to parrots. You must either use cookware without nonstick surfaces, or keep your parrot in a well-ventilated area away from these dangerous fumes. Other things that might commonly be in the air that will harm a parrot are hairspray, spray deodorant, air fresheners, scented candles, perfume, and cigarette smoke. Make sure to keep these things far away from your pet.

Grooming Your Parrot

Believe it or not, most parrots love baths, showers, or gentle sprays from misting bottles. In fact, parrots need occasional baths or showers to stay clean and healthy. Parrot feathers give off a powder or dust that protects and cleans their feathers. But that means parrots must bathe in order to

This parrot enjoys having water sprayed gently from a spray bottle.

keep the right amount of feather dust in their feathers. Some parrot owners put a shower rod across the bathtub so their parrot has its own perch in the shower! Using a gentle shower spray helps keep you parrot's skin and feathers clean and healthy. But showers have another benefit: the humidity in a warm shower or bath helps keep a parrot's breathing parts clear and moist. Depending on your parrot's particular personality, some parrots prefer gentle misting from a spray bottle. You can also offer a shallow dish—the base of a ceramic flower pot works well—so your parrot can splash around on its own.

Molting

About once a year, parrots go through a molting process. When a parrot molts, it replaces its feathers with new ones. As new feathers—called **pin feathers**—grow in, the old feathers fall out. But it does not happen all at once. Usually, parrots molt a few feathers at a time. Growing feathers are sometimes called "blood feathers" because the **quill**—the hollow shaft that runs down the middle of a feather—has a blood supply to enrich the fast-growing feather. When the feather is done growing, the blood supply is sealed off. If you have a pet parrot that is molting, do not disturb the new feathers because a broken blood feather can cause a parrot to bleed a lot.

Molting parrots will preen often. As new feathers grow in, they are cloaked in a protective sheath that flakes off as the feather grows. Preening helps this process along. Although your parrot is replacing its feathers, it should not have bald spots, since new feathers force old feathers out. If your parrot has bald spots, it might be sick. Bring your parrot to the vet if you notice bald spots.

When parrots molt in the wild, other parrots help them preen the molting feathers on its head and neck. If you have a single parrot, you can help your molting parrot by increasing its showers to help the parrot shed the protective covering on its new feathers. Some owners help single parrots preen the pin feathers on its neck and head, but it is important not to do this too early. If a pin feather is preened before the blood supply is sealed off, it can cause the parrot to bleed a lot. Ask your parrot's vet if it seems like your parrot needs help preening during molting.

As your bird gets used to you, it may ask to have parts of its head, neck, or back rubbed gently. Whenever you pet your bird, be careful of pin and blood feathers that are just coming in.

Sometimes when a parrot is unhappy, lonely, or stressed out, it will begin to pluck its own feathers out. If your pet parrot starts to pull its feathers out, consult your vet to find out what changes your parrot's lifestyle might need.

Clipped Wings

Some parrot owners clip the ends of their birds' wings so that they cannot fly. This prevents a parrot from taking flight indoors and potentially hurting itself by flying into a window, ceiling fan, onto a hot stove, or from flying out open doors or windows. Ask the breeder or your parrot's vet how to trim wing feathers. The best methods involve leaving enough feather so the parrot can fly short distances, but trimming enough so it cannot gain a lot of height or speed. When done correctly, it does not hurt the parrot, and the feathers will grow back. Always have an adult help you trim your parrot's wings.

Your parrot's nails will also have to be cut or filed down. Ask a breeder or veterinarian to show you how to safely do this.

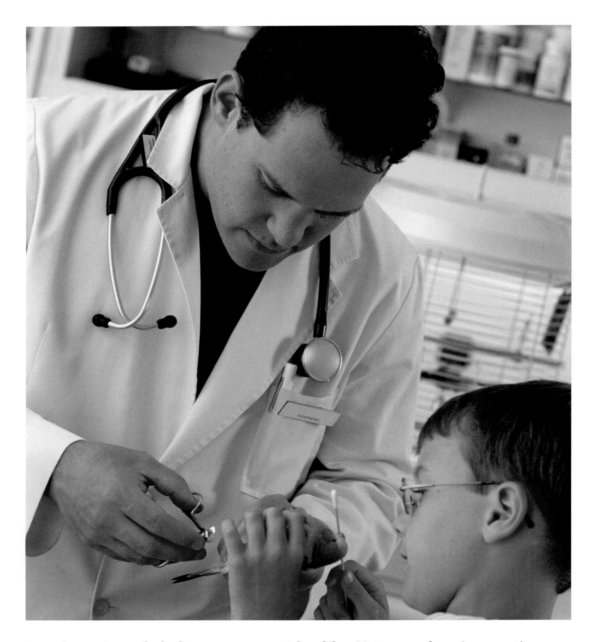

An avian vet can help keep your parrot healthy. Vets can also give you tips on how to groom your parrot.

When to See a Vet

When you first get your new parrot, you should bring it to a veterinarian to make sure it is healthy. Not every vet has the special knowledge to care for a parrot, so look for an avian veterinarian, which is a vet that specializes in taking care of birds. Your parrot's vet will give you a lot of information about the best ways to care for your parrot's specific species, and how often to bring your parrot for check-ups. The vet might take blood samples or samples of your parrot's droppings to test for diseases. In addition, you should bring your parrot to the vet if it seems sick. Sick parrots sometimes show less appetite and playfulness, they may sleep more than usual or sit with their feathers fluffed out. Sick parrots might sneeze, yawn a lot, or have vomiting or diarrhea. If you suspect your parrot may be sick, call the vet.

Training Your Parrot

Parrots are very intelligent animals, and many can be trained to perform a variety of tricks. Parrots are perhaps most famous for their ability to mimic sound, or "talk." But a parrot can also be trained to step onto your hand, go back to its cage, wave with a wing or foot, nod its head "yes" or shake its head "no," and even do simple puzzles.

Training a parrot requires patience and planning. Parrots respond to positive rewards for good behavior, rather than negative actions for bad behavior. For example, to train your parrot to step up to your hand, you might give it a treat when it does what you want it to do. However, it is not helpful for training to punish the bird if it does not do what you want it to do. Good treats for training parrots might be fruit, nuts, or its favorite type of seed.

Socializing Your Parrot

Parrots need to interact with humans from an early age in order to be good pets. When parrots are used to being around people, they can form a bond with humans similar to the bonds many dogs have with their owners. Some parrots have been known to snuggle with their humans! Often, parrots will form this bond with the main person who cares for it. However, parrots that have not had a lot of contact with humans from a very young age will be happiest living with another pet parrot for company. Whether you have one bird or two, good socialization is very important.

Good socialization includes handling, or holding, your parrot a lot. Your parrot should learn to come out of its cage voluntarily. You should never have to reach in and grab your parrot. Many parrots are trained to come out of their cages by stepping onto their owner's finger, hand, or arm. Training your parrot to come out to you takes time and a lot of patience. Once your parrot is comfortably perched it may be happy to rest there, while preening, playing, or eating. Some parrots like to perch on their owners' shoulders or heads. Only allow this if you are sure that your parrot will not bite or scratch your ears or face. If your parrot likes to perch on your shoulder, be sure to remove any earrings or small hair clips that can be picked off by a sharp beak!

Playful Parrots

Parrots should be given a variety of toys to play with. Toys help parrots satisfy their natural curiosity and playfulness. Plus, it helps them pass the time when their humans are busy doing other things. Look for toys made with natural wood or rope. A parrot will chew its toys, so for larger parrots, avoid plastic or any metal other than stainless steel. (Some smaller parrots can

Parrots enjoy playing with their toys. With patience and treats, some parrots can be taught to do tricks with their toys.

have toys made of sturdy plastic.) Just like us, parrots will grow bored with playing with the same toys over and over, so introduce new toys every so often to keep your parrot active and occupied.

Parrots also often enjoy sitting on their own perch outside their cage. A T-stand—a perch on a pole—lets your parrot know it has its own spot in the house. It also gives your parrot an alternative to perching on dangerous or valuable things in the house, like curtain rods, lamps, or furniture. A parrot outside its cage must be supervised at all times to make sure it does not get hurt. Also, make sure no windows or doors are open so you can avoid a parrot chase through your neighborhood!

Parrots can be majestic in their grand, colorful beauty, awe-inspiring in their intelligence, and cherished for the bonds they can form with humans. Keeping your parrot healthy and happy takes time, but the reward is a long life of parrot companionship that is worth the effort.

With patience and care, you and your feathered friend can spend many happy years together.

Glossary

avian—A term that refers to birds.

blood feathers—Developing feathers that contain a blood supply that helps the feather grow quickly.

breeder—Someone who raises parrots to be sold as pets.

crest—A tuft of feathers on the heads of some types of parrots, especially certain varieties of cockatoos.

mimic—To imitate something, such as a sound or a word.

molting—The process through which parrots grow new feathers to replace old feathers.

pin feathers—New feathers that grow in during the molting process.

preening—The act of a parrot grooming its feathers.

quill—The hollow structure that runs down a feather's center.

veterinarian—A doctor that treats animals. Veterinarians that specialize in birds are called avian veterinarians.

Find Out More

Books

Athan, Mattie Sue. *Parrots: A Complete Pet Owner's Manual.* Hauppauge, NY: Barron's Educational Series, 2002.

Barnes, Julia. *Pet Parakeets.* Milwaukee, WI: Gareth Stevens, 2007.

Low, Rosemary. *The Parrot Companion: Caring for Parrots, Macaws, Budgies, Cockatiels and More.* Buffalo, NY: Firefly Books, 2006.

Web Sites

The World Parrot Trust
http://www.parrots.org
The World Parrot Trust is a charitable organization dedicated to conserving parrots in the wild, as well as working for the welfare of pet parrots. The site features an "ask the expert" area, a large parrot encyclopedia, articles about the responsibilities of keeping a pet parrot, and a lot more.

The Association of Avian Veterinarians

http://www.aav.org/vet-lookup

In this Web site, you can find a vet that is specifically trained to care for parrots and other types of birds.

The Avian Welfare Coalition

http://www.avianwelfare.org

The Avian Welfare Coalition offers information about how to care for parrots, places to adopt pet parrots (organized by state), a lost and found page for missing or found birds, and other resources.

Foster Parrots Ltd.

http://www.fosterparrots.com

Foster Parrots is a rescue organization and sanctuary in Massachusetts, but their Web site has a lot of valuable parrot information for parrot lovers. Topics include how to care for parrots, recipes for parrot-safe household cleaners, tips for finding an escaped bird, and free posters and postcards you can print on a computer.

Index

Page numbers for illustrations are in **bold.**

About the Author

Johannah Haney is a freelance writer, and has written several books for Marshall Cavendish Benchmark. She lives in Boston with her husband, Andrés, and their two cats.